To Never Give Up!

A Single Mother's Courageous Stand To Triumph Over Tragedy

Debra T. Pickett

Copyright © 2014 by Debra T. Pickett

To Never Give Up!
A Single Mother's Courageous Stand To Triumph Over Tragedy
by Debra T. Pickett

Printed in the United States of America

ISBN 9781498406307

All rights reserved solely by the author. The author guarantees all contents are original and do not infringe upon the legal rights of any other person or work. No portion of this publication may be reproduced, stored in any electronic system, or transmitted in any form or by any means, electronic, mechanical, photocopy, recording, or otherwise, without written permission from the author. Brief quotations may be used in literary reviews. The views expressed in this book are not necessarily those of the publisher.

Scripture quotations taken from the New King James Version (NKJV) of the Holy Bible. Copyright © 1996, 2004, 2007 by Tyndale House Foundation. Used by permission. All rights reserved.

www.xulonpress.com

"For God has not given us a spirit of fear, but of power and of love and of a sound mind."

~ 2 Timothy 1:7

To Never Give Up!

*A Single Mother's Courageous Stand
to Triumph over Tragedy*

Table of Contents

Part I ~ How It All Began 19
Part II ~ Shattered Dreams 35
Part III ~ Like A Butterfly 49
Part IV ~ Marred & Mangled, But Making It 59
Part V ~ To Never Give Up! 77

FOREWORD

Now more than ever before, it is IMPORTANT for parents to sacrifice in order to raise intelligent, healthy, and whole children. Based on statistics and on our declining economy, single parenting is on the rise. Oftentimes, single parents feel overwhelmed and inundated with all of life's responsibilities, including raising children on limited budgets. Today's youth are facing many pressures: gangs, drugs, teenage promiscuity, and a myriad of other societal problems.

Regardless of today's reality, there are some very powerful parents who are doing the best they can to raise successful and responsible children. This book is for the parent who oftentimes feels overwhelmed... for the parent who has considered giving up and giving in. With God and a few quality individuals that He puts in our path, it is possible to overcome life's obstacles.

In *To Never Give Up!* Debra Pickett shares her story of difficulties, challenges, and triumphs. At the point of losing it all, she clung to her faith and did not give up. Single-handedly raising four well-rounded young men, she has a story to tell. Debra has proven that with faith in God, never giving up on herself and her dreams, and lots of hard work, it is possible in this day and time to raise obedient and God-fearing, male children. This book is a MUST READ for all parents, especially those who have contemplated giving up.

Dwayne Bryant, President
Inner-Vision International

DEDICATION

This book is dedicated to individuals everywhere who have ever said:

- *"I can't do this anymore!"*
- *"This isn't worth it!"*
- *"I don't know who I am anymore!"*
- *"Why me? Why this?! Why now?!!"*
- *"I'm done!"*
- *"My life isn't worth living."*

You know what? You're absolutely right!

- You can't do this anymore because something greater is designed for you!
- This isn't worth it because it's worth so much more; it is priceless, to be exact!
- It's great you don't know who you are anymore because now you can get to know WHOSE you are. You are royalty!
- Why you? Because no one has your skills, gifts, talents, or beauty! Why this? Because this is the perfect accessory needed to bring out your bright eyes of hope, your pure heart of love, and your sound mind filled with wisdom! Why now? Because the Creator's set time to favor you is NOW!
- You're done. Great! Now, it's time for those who've been waiting on you to experience your goodness and gifts!
- Your life isn't just worth living; it's worth CELEBRATING!

ACKNOWLEDGMENTS

To my God, my Savior, my Guide
To my Sons:
Byron, Jr.
Nicholas
Justin
Caleb

PROLOGUE

My eyes suddenly flew open in the hot, dark room. I could hear the fan we all shared whirring as it cycled toward my door. I reached for my cell phone. It was exactly 1:29 a.m. on July 20, 2011, and something wasn't right. My first thought was, "Oh no! I'm about to have another panic attack!" But as I sat up on the side of my bed, my legs and knees still throbbing with pain from a car accident I had been involved in just a month earlier, I realized it wasn't another panic attack. Then it hit me! I was supposed to have recertified for my unemployment benefits on the day before and totally forgot! *Then I panicked.* What was I going to do? How could I be so forgetful? I felt like the biggest screw-up. "Why, God?!" I silently cried out, so as to not wake the boys. "How could I forget something so important and so needed? I need that money for rent. I'm already late and had promised to have it this weekend! What do I do?!"

I left my bedroom and went into the bathroom, where I just stared at myself in the mirror. What's happening to me? What has happened to my life? How in the world did I end up here, and how am I going to come out of this? No job; no transportation; no real home; **NO MORE!**

Back in my bedroom as I sat in the dark, a myriad of thoughts zipped across my mind. I spoke quietly to myself, "This is it." And then I began to pray for all the host of heaven to please come and help me. I had no more strength or the will to fight another battle. This was as far as I could go. Then I thought about my sons: four wonderful, young men. I've given them all I have to give....I'll tell them today...they are on their own with God now. He'll help them and guide them throughout their lives.

    I picked up my cell phone. It was now after 4 a.m., and, after 18 years of heartaches, setbacks, struggles, challenges, and many emotional and physical battles, ***I was ready to give up.***

PART I

HOW IT ALL BEGAN

*"Before I formed you in the womb I knew you;
Before you were born I sanctified you..."
~ Jeremiah 1:5*

1

*E*ver since I could remember, I've heard the story of my birth told many times. My oldest brother, Laserik, who at about three years old kept telling our parents: *"I see Jesus in the clouds! Can't you see Him? He's right there!"* Like any other determined three-year-old, Laserik was very upset that our parents could not see what he could see. He excitedly announced, *"Jesus has a sister for me named Terese, and she's coming for my birthday!"*

Needless to say, something so profound repeatedly coming from a three-year-old is not to be ignored. So, as the story goes, on June 27th the following year, I was born. My arrival home from the hospital on July 3rd coincided with Laserik's fourth birthday.

According to family history, I cried a lot, much to the annoyance of my older brother. He later told my parents that Jesus had sent the wrong baby and asked whether they could take me back and get the right one! So began my life . . . with tears and rejection.

Growing up knowing that your birth was the manifestation of a fulfilled prophecy is quite a load for a young girl to bear. I became self-conscious about who I was and what I was supposed to do and wished to remain anonymous and invisible for the rest of my life. To make matters worse, I began having visions of myself, as an adult, speaking before many people. I couldn't understand this, so I kept it to myself so as not to seem more "different" than I had already been labeled. I constantly struggled with learning to accept myself for who I was without regard to what others thought or felt about me. I soon became an *overachiever* and a *people-pleaser*. I settled for going through the motions of maintaining compliant relationships with others by being as obedient of a child as I could; this would keep others happy. But the frustration in me was building.

I often escaped the pressure by burying myself in reading. This was my escape from reality. At the age of 15 I could not "take *it* anymore." It seemed as though everyone had high expectations for me, and I was convinced that I could not continue to fulfill their hopes and dreams for my life while not really acknowledging my own hopes and dreams With the mounting pressures looming, I attempted to take my life.

The details of how I attempted to end my life are not as important as noting that many people have come to this point of frustration where they just want to end it all and be done with life. But, the important thing to know is that ending life here on Earth is only beginning it in eternity. No matter how bad things appear, suicide is never the true solution to anyone's life problems. Eternal judgment is no match for temporary discomfort and chaos. Things will get better sooner than you think. To "end it all" is nothing more than a trick solution of our greatest enemy because he knows your victorious success equals the demise of his reign in your life!

Through this experience, I came to *know* the Lord Jesus as my personal Savior and Friend. I had been born and raised in the Pentecostal church. I knew all the books of the Bible, the 23rd Psalm, the Beatitudes, and the Ten Commandments among other scriptures and the church doctrine. I faithfully attended Sunday school, sang in the choir, helped in the kitchen, volunteered during Vacation Bible School, and even worked as a junior camp counselor at the St. Luke Summer Day Camp. I had learned the "religion" but had never experienced a *"relationship."* This was a new and grand experience for me, especially as a teenager.

I often think about how much I would have missed out on had I actually ended my life. There are people who have reached what they think is their point of no return, when in reality they have reached the threshold of a brand new beginning. A new beginning means a new seed has been planted. Have you ever planted a flower seed? It looks nothing like the picture on the package, does it? In fact, you may even doubt that such a tiny seed could really develop into such a beautiful specimen. However, because of your belief in what the package portrays, you go ahead and plant the seed believing that what you have read on the package will grow at the appointed time if you care for the seed according to the instructions.

As it is with flowering seeds, so it is with us. We are seeds planted in this Earth. We sometimes doubt that the person we see in the mirror could ever be victorious, beautiful, talented, healthy, and wealthy. The Word of God is the package that reveals who we are to become in life. We need only to initiate the same amount of faith it took to plant the flower seed. Believe what the Word of God says about who we are and what we are to become! If we care for ourselves and obey the Word of God, then at the appointed time, we will see the manifestation of the power of God revealed in our lives!

The purpose of a seed is to continue to produce more of its kind as long as the Earth exists. Within a particular seed is everything it is to become, and its development in the right environment will produce the desired result.

2

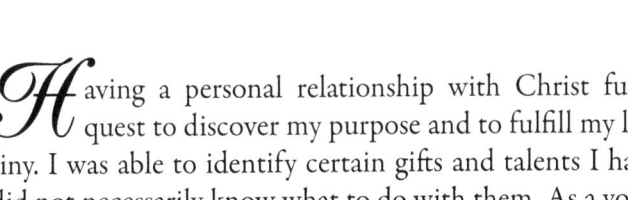

Having a personal relationship with Christ fueled my quest to discover my purpose and to fulfill my life's destiny. I was able to identify certain gifts and talents I had, but I did not necessarily know what to do with them. As a young girl, I began to feel a strong urge to find out what my name "*Terese*" meant. Why did the Lord choose this name for me versus some other name? Through much searching, I found out it came from a Greek word that means "summer" or "harvest." I knew about harvesting or reaping crops from some of the books I had read, but what, if anything, did this have to do with me?

During my teenaged years, my Dad kept a small garden in our backyard. Since I always felt a special connection to nature and since this work coincided with the meaning of my name, I appointed myself as his assistant gardener and made it my duty to daily care for the collard greens, banana and jalapeño peppers, and tomatoes that he would plant. As I tended the vegetables, the Holy Spirit often spoke to me of the frailty and the harmony of nature.

Rain, soil, and sunlight, things created and supplied naturally by God, ensured proper conditions for the vegetables' growth. A skilled gardener was also needed to nurture the vegetables to help ensure successful growth. If I wasn't careful, overwatering could drown the plants or cause damage to the vegetables. Being too anxious to pick them wouldn't allow them to fully develop, thus affecting the taste and nutrition they could provide. Not knowing the difference between a weed and the plant itself would jeopardize the life and fruit of the vine. Carelessly administering insecticides designed to kill harmful bugs could adversely affect the health of those who ate the vegetables. In other words, everything in life has to fulfill a designated process to achieve its ultimate purpose, but negligence can destroy its intended development.

It was my father who initially planted the vegetable seeds, but it was both of us working together with nature to provide proper care that caused the vegetables to grow. When it came time to pick the vegetables, after explaining to me how I would know which ones were ripe for picking, my Dad allowed me the honor of doing the actual "harvesting." After picking the greens, tomatoes, and peppers, I washed them and helped my mother use them to prepare delicious meals for our family.

Through this experience, the Lord began to show me, not so much of what my purpose was, but how I was *connected* to Him. I learned firsthand that He *is* a loving Father who longs for a relationship with his children. Before we can **do** anything for the Lord, we must first **be** relationally connected to Him.

Spiritually speaking, I was now beginning to understand that "my" life's purpose was not really "mine" at all but more of a fulfillment of God's intention for my life. Without the Lord doing His part, all that we do is in vain. This entire gardening experience with my Dad caused me to begin to really seek to know more about the Lord and His will for my life. I sought God in a new and different way. I began to read the Bible for understanding and application. As I grew into a young adult, my relationship with the Lord began to flourish. I prayed diligently for many things: direction for college attendance, employment, and even marriage. I was learning how to trust in the Lord for myself. I was not always embraced by the in-crowd among my peers, but because of my conscientious lifestyle as a Christian, I was well respected. I was finally reaping the benefits of living my life according to the will of God. After earning a college degree and securing employment in my chosen field of work, I began to desire to be married and raise a family.

I purposed in my 21-year-old heart that I would marry a man who loved the Lord with all his heart, soul, mind, and strength; who had solid employment, preferably his own business; who was financially secure and stable; and who would love me unconditionally. So, when I became acquainted with my future spouse, I was ecstatic! He *seemed* to be "The One." Besides, he came from a family that had grown up in the same church as I had and our extended families had a long, solid, and connected past, which began in the south. Despite our 10-year age difference, this seemed better than perfect. So, on October 10, 1992, at the age of 23, I married and was living on top of the world! My purpose was truly unfolding in what I thought was the most glorious way.

3

The beginning of anything in our lives, especially our life itself, is the most critical time of development. This is also true of marriage. It takes a daily display of honesty, commitment to the wedding vows, undying love, and, more importantly, love for Christ to ensure that a strong marital foundation is established. When these things are consistently lacking or missing all together, the marriage is headed for trouble. Such was the case of my marriage. After just a few weeks of being married, I begin to experience telling signs that something was definitely amiss. I scolded myself for being a worry wart and for making too much ado about nothing. In essence, I ignored the signs of marital dysfunction. I didn't want to believe that my dream life was heading downhill, so I fought hard to make it work. I focused on my work and began to nurse the new life that I discovered was growing inside me.

When I found out I was expecting our first child I was so ecstatic (and deathly afraid) that I was going to have a baby! I assumed that it was going to be a girl because, between our two families, girls were the dominant siblings. I began speaking to the baby as if I were addressing a daughter. But only a few weeks into the pregnancy I began spotting, which signaled that I was threatening a miscarriage. I sought emergency medical attention and was emphatically warned by my obstetrician that immediate bed rest was most important if I wanted to deliver a full-term, healthy baby. This meant no work, no shopping, and no visiting. I was to do NOTHING but REST!

It was during this time that I really began to pray for the child within me. In the midst of my praying, a still, small voice spoke the words, "*It's a boy.*" Whoa!!! With this new revelation, I began to pray for our *son*. Within a few weeks, when I went back to my obstetrician for a checkup, I was told that all was well and that the baby was fine. Hallelujah! I could not help but think about what was really going on in this situation. I was declaring the opposite of what the Lord wanted to manifest within me, so much so, that I was in danger of speaking death on my *promised* blessing. You see, I had forgotten that when I was a teenager, because I loved playing softball so much, I prayed fervently and asked the Lord that if I ever grew up and got married that I wanted nine sons so that I could form my own team! After my third son, I adjusted my petition concerning children. God had remembered my prayer request and was in the midst of honoring what I desired in my heart. I was the one who got caught up and begin to desire something other than what He had already designed for me.

Some of us are declaring things over our lives that God never ordained for us and we're wondering why and where all the trouble and chaos are coming from. The only way I was able to hear the revelation from the Lord regarding my son was when I *obeyed* the doctor's orders and when I *became still* before the Lord. I was then in a position to inquire of the Lord regarding my situation. And since I remained in that place *patiently,* I was able to hear and receive my answer. Being obedient and following direction from the Lord can literally save our lives. If I had disobeyed and did what I wanted to do, I would not have been blessed with an aspiring master musician in the person of Byron, Jr.!

4

Our family was rapidly growing: we went from two becoming one to four in a little less than three years with the birth of our second son, Nicholas. Marital challenges continued to mount, as well. A joint decision between my spouse and me even before the boys were born was that I would be a stay-at-home mom so that I could raise them as I had been reared, giving our children a strong foundation. Since this was a joint decision, I expected total support from my spouse; however, that was not the case.

While marital troubles continued to escalate, so did my prayer life. By the time I was expecting our third child, I was becoming more upset with the condition of our marriage. Because of the inability to communicate with my spouse, I took to holding everything in. This became my coping mechanism for the duration of my marriage. It did not matter what I did to make things comfortable, nothing was ever good enough. My prayers became debates with the Lord. I wanted Him to explain to me what in the world was going on because I was not happy and **He** needed to know!

Our third son, Justin, was born in the middle of a snowstorm. Upon his delivery, I could feel that something was not right. I heard no cry. What I did hear was my obstetrician yelling at the nurses for emergency equipment to be brought in. When I looked up, I saw the umbilical cord wrapped twice around his neck. His little hand was holding it as if he were trying to pull it off.

Everyone started rushing around, all the while I kept asking, "What's happening to my baby?! Is he alright?!" Finally I heard him cry. Then I cried. My obstetrician explained to me that Justin had been born with infant pneumonia and would need to stay in the special care nursery. I visited with him as often as I could while recuperating in the hospital but then was told that I had to leave him at the hospital until he was better. I had to go home without our son. Needless to say, initially I was inconsolable then I heard a familiar voice assure me that the baby would be fine. I was able to go home in peace and rest up for his arrival a week later.

While recuperating at home, the Lord began to show me how my emotional state during my pregnancy impacted the baby's birth. I held all my pain, frustration, fear, and hurt inside, which caused undue stress on the baby. He could feel what I was feeling. As I wrestled with the entangled cords of an unfulfilled marriage, my son was wrestling with a tangled umbilical cord. All of my debates with the Lord, I later learned, impacted his personality and character in such a way that I teasingly call him my "great debater"; ever since he was big enough to talk, his main mode of communication has been to debate.

I just knew that after this very stressful time that the state of my marriage would greatly improve. I wanted to believe that the Lord was using this situation to touch my spouse's heart so that he would be the man God was calling him to be. I can't say how wrong I was. As a matter fact, the very next year when I gave birth to my fourth and final son, Caleb, financial troubles were so prevalent that we were without a home, I didn't know where I was going to live when I left the hospital. The stress this put on me as a young mother with four babies all under the age of five was almost unbearable. However, my faith in God prompted me to trust Him to provide for us; and, of course, He came through by providing a place for us to live. I often thought how strange it was that the most wonderful experiences in my life were coupled with some of the worst experiences in my life.

The giddiness and excitement of being newly married was coupled with discovering inconsistencies and misgivings in my marriage. Giving birth to four wonderful and handsome sons within the course of five years was coupled with the slow disintegration of our nuclear family—something I never dreamed would happen to me. It was this unraveling of my marriage that defined the next phase of my life and led me into a deeper search for true purpose in my life.

PART II

Shattered Dreams

"Trust in the Lord with all your heart, And lean not on your own understanding; In all your ways acknowledge Him, And He shall direct your paths."

~Proverbs 3:5-6

5

When things in your life begin to progress in a direction that you never intended them to go, God is still able to keep you. My expectations of having a Godly marriage quickly began to fade. I always held the sanctity of marriage with high regard because of its comparison in the Bible to Christ's love for His Church. I truly desired for my marriage to be the perfect earthly replica. I wasn't expecting it to be a bed of roses, but I felt that since both my spouse and I were professing salvation, there would be nothing we would not be able to overcome. The important thing to note here is that I assumed that our individual relationship with and commitment to the Lord were in some way equal. I thought that when things got really difficult, we would be able to put our personal differences aside and seek God's will in whatever we faced, no matter what. Unfortunately, again, this was not the case. One night, I had a very telling dream regarding the state of my marriage:

I was standing in the lobby of my former church dressed in complete wedding attire waiting for the wedding to take place. Prior to this, I had been busy making sure everything was in order so that the ceremony could begin. Some of our guests were walking around in blue jeans and T-shirts, eating pizza and barbecue. I became very upset and began asking for my spouse. As I turned around, he was standing behind me dressed in his work clothes, looking disheveled.

I asked him why he wasn't dressed. He looked at me and answered nonchalantly, "I am dressed. All of that isn't necessary."

I woke from this dream very troubled because it seemed so real. When I had this dream I had been married for close to six years. I then remembered that during our premarital counseling we were given an assignment to read the 13th chapter of 1 Corinthians and describe how we would exhibit each attribute of love in our marriage. Well, being who I was, I worked diligently on the assignment as if it were a college level research paper. On the other hand, my soon-to-be-husband completed only part of the assignment. What our pastor shared with him was that if he didn't complete the assignment before the wedding, this would prove what kind of commitment he would have to me and our marriage. He would go only so far in the marriage and leave the bulk of the responsibility to me. Profoundly and unfortunately, that revelation bore true. The dream confirmed the reality of our separate commitments to the marriage.

I sought the Lord diligently for guidance in maintaining my role in the marriage. I continued to abide faithfully by keeping a clean home, homeschooling the children, drawing my spouse's bath, occasionally cutting his hair, baking his favorite cakes, cooking his favorite meals, doing the laundry, and performing other marital duties. Unfortunately, none of this was good enough.

I had no access to our finances and many times the children and I were left to depend on family and friends to assist with daily necessities. For about two months, I couldn't sleep in my bedroom. I slept on a pallet in my living room with CeCe Winans's *Throne Room* CD playing through the night. My strength began to fail miserably. I became depressed and battled with low self-esteem from the verbal and emotional abuse I suffered. I sought no help from anyone because by this time, who could I really trust for the kind of support I needed? I continued to rely on God's strength and help.

I had to go back to work in order to support myself but ended up having to pay all household bills, too, because "no one told me to go to work." Being placed in this position exhausted any monies I made from working. What I endured, I was told, was my fault for trying to "do stuff."

Driving home from work on the expressway one day, my car began to shake violently. I was able to make it to the right shoulder. An IDOT truck driver happened to see me and pulled up behind me. After checking my car, he asked me who had been working on my car. I told him no one. He asked whether I was sure, and I told him I was quite sure. Then he told me that all the lug nuts on the tire on the front passenger side were loosened to the point where I could've ended up "spread across the expressway." After he pulled off, with tears running down my face, I began to praise the Lord for sparing my life.

In all this, I never stopped being a faithful wife. I'm not going to give you the impression that I was perfect. I struggled much with anger, bitterness, resentment, shame, and guilt; especially since I didn't know to whom to go to for help. After all, I did all the *right* things early on to make sure I would have a fulfilling life. So how did I end up in this dysfunctional marriage? For what was I being punished?!

During these times, the lakefront became a place of solace, refuge, and peace for me. I would wait until my spouse was sound asleep, and, during the wee hours of some Saturday mornings, I would go to the lakefront and walk, pray, read my Word, and write in my journal. After two hours of that, I was strong enough to deal with whatever came my way. It was during these times that the Lord began to teach me to speak His Words over my life. Before then, I would just accept whatever words and actions came my way, be it from others or myself. Words, positive or negative, are seeds that can be manifested in our lives. Everything we speak will bring forth in abundance. Choose wisely!

Although difficult for me to share, the reality of what I endured is meant to deliver and strengthen someone else in similar or worse circumstances, whether male or female. While the previous events were part of a hurtful past, forgiveness has influenced healing and growth. The message here is that if the Lord allows you to come to it, He'll certainly bring you through it!

6

I did my very best to shield my children from the unfolding disaster taking place under our roof. I panicked when they begin to question things they heard and saw when not in my presence. Of all I endured, this was the most heartbreaking for me. I had always taught my boys to pray for their father. I never spoke ill about him to them. I told them that no matter what happened he was still their father and according to the Word of God, they had to honor and respect him. "Only God can change someone's heart; we can only show them love," I would constantly explain.

I always honored the concerns of my children. I never brushed them off as unimportant. Although these times were difficult for them, it was also a learning opportunity. They could learn how not to be when they became men; and I could teach them early how to wisely deal with difficult situations in their lives. We had many discussions about life and how God factors in with how we live our lives on a daily basis. Mind you, my boys were not yet teenagers; they were all younger than eight years old. With all the negative experiences, I didn't hesitate to remind them of the good things their father did, as well, like fix on cars, and play video games with them.

Because their father was gone a lot, I made sure they had plenty of opportunity to just be boys. I purchased a softball, baseball bat, basketball, football, and bikes; many days we hung out at the park or lakefront; and yes, I played, too! At home, we read books, watched movies, and played board games as well as computer and video games.

I let them cook and bake with me because they needed to learn these skills for when they would one day be on their own. Besides, we treated it like science experiments, and sometimes it was.

It was important for me to expose them to different environments that would promote their healthy growth and development. I was never able to travel with them as I desired, but we visited museums, zoos, and libraries and participated in community and church events whenever we could. When their father came home during the week while we were out somewhere, he was always invited to join us. Sometimes this made for much grumbling, but I was determined to teach them what showing love was really about. I explained that we all grow from the inside out and growing in love is just as important as growing up in age and size. This is a lesson we all must learn.

Just as we grow physically, we also grow spiritually, emotionally, socially, and mentally. We grow in proportion to our surroundings. If our surroundings are limited, then our growth will be limited. It's easy to recognize the physical or outward changes, but have you also considered the inward changes? Isn't it amazing that this change takes place holistically and not just in one area of our lives?

Take a good look at yourself in the nearest mirror. What do you see? Certainly it's not the same individual that stared back at you 10, 20, or even 30 years ago! What has changed? Look at your hands. When did you notice your hands had grown bigger? Or had you even stopped to pay attention? How did they get bigger? I'll tell you. Something was, and still is, happening on the **inside** of you that is causing your outward self to change.

I'm reminded of a story I heard once about a man who purchased exotic fish for a brand new fish tank he had in his office. After having the fish for a few months, he could not comprehend why his fish were not as large as the ones he had observed at the pet shop. It was during a visit from an old friend that the man was enlightened about the lack of physical development of his fish. The friend explained that the fish would only grow as big as the tank in which they were placed. If the man would place them in a bigger fish tank, the fish would grow to their proper size. The man took the wise counsel of his friend and within a few months' time, he noticed the fish were getting larger. Just like the fish in the man's tank, our true growth and development can be hindered by our limited environment.

Unlike the fish, however, we are able to change our environment in order to promote healthy growth and development in our lives. This takes strength, courage, and faith, but it is possible to achieve! I know because in our home, things had progressed to such a threatening degree that I had to change environments.

7

There are circumstances that can challenge our vision for the future, but God has already provided a way for us to escape hopelessness and despair. Although I had never planned on my marriage ending in divorce, I was faced with the reality that it was over. With prayer and fasting, I sought the Lord for an answer. I refused to move until I knew I was hearing from the Lord. Then it happened in a way and at a time that I never expected. I was awakened out of my sleep one morning at 3 o'clock to find information that threatened our peace and safety. I knew immediately it was time to move.

The Lord used a small but memorable moment to prompt me to move forward. It was on a Sunday after our noon service that I went to speak to my Aunt Mary, my mother's oldest sister. Aunt Mary was a very devout, prim, and proper woman. Over the years, we often had conversations about living holy, sewing, and using our gifts and talents for the Lord. As we sat and chatted, she asked me about my marriage. I just shook my head and told her, in a shaky voice, that, given the state of things, I really didn't think it would last much longer. I fought hard to hold back tears. She looked at me, crossed her leg (which shocked me, if you knew Aunt Mary), cleared her throat, and said, "Debbie, what you need is a strategy. You see, we can't change people and when they don't want to change, you have to do what's best for you and the children. Just pray and ask the Lord to show you what to do. He will. Then you let the Lord deal with the man."

I did just what Aunt Mary said. And with guidance from the Lord, we were packed and ready to move one month later. The only hindrance was that we were left with no one to help us move. It's not that I hadn't arranged for help in advance; my help reneged on moving day. So here we were, all packed and ready to move forward but stuck. Did the Lord not mean for me to go? Had I misunderstood? No way! If that was the case, I would not have been able to secure an apartment. That alone had been a miracle.

I went to my room and lay across my bed. The tears flowed. I told the Lord that I had done all that He told me to do throughout this entire ordeal and that I couldn't understand why we were stranded. I felt like the children of Israel when Moses led them from Egypt to the Red Sea, and they turned and saw Pharaoh and his army closely pursuing them. I knew that it was either move now or face "Pharaoh;" if I had to face "Pharaoh," then my life was over. I no longer had strength to endure any more abuse. It was then that the Spirit of God reminded me of something He had told me eight years earlier:

I was in my last trimester of pregnancy with our last son. In the wee hours of the morning, I heard a voice telling me to "Go down to the potter's house." It was so clear and distinct; I thought my spouse was talking in his sleep. I sat up in bed and waited to see if I would hear him say something else. What I did hear was the same voice repeating the same words. This time it sounded as if the person was directly in front of me. I knew then that it was the Lord. So I reluctantly rolled out of bed, grabbed my Bible, and headed downstairs to the living room. I sank slowly to my knees at the couch and opened my Bible to the passage in Jeremiah (chapter 18) that speaks of the potter's house. As I began to read, the Spirit of the Lord dealt with me about my life up to that point. He explained that while serving the Lord and being obedient to His will, I had become marred by way of ill-treatment from people whom I had held in high esteem, so much so that my service to Him had been deeply affected. I found it difficult to continue serving the Lord with the same motivation and fervency as I had before. For me, my service to the Lord encompassed all areas of my life: as a wife, a mother, a friend, a Sunday school teacher, an evangelist, etc. My life was my ministry. All these areas became affected as I began to suffer. So much of Him had already been worked into my life; rather than leave me to live my life in such a broken condition, barely able to perform according to His will, He promised to make me over into another vessel. He lovingly let me know He would transform me into something more valuable than I already was.

The word of the Lord states in verse four of Jeremiah 18 that "...the vessel that he made of clay was marred in the hand of the potter; so he made it again into another vessel, as it seemed good to the potter to make." There were so many different types of vessels that this potter could have transformed this work into, but the new vessel would have to reflect the level of relationship he had already invested into it. He did not want to start from scratch and ignore all the emotion and love and commitment that he had invested. The potter wanted the transformed work to reflect the value of his heart and his hand, so making any old thing just wouldn't suffice; a special work was now in progress. In other words, I would experience a lifestyle change. In the meantime, I was to just submit to His process. I was also told that I would have a Red Sea experience in my life and when the time came, I was to just trust God for deliverance.

Being reminded that the Lord was about to do something new and different in my life was something that I did not know how to accept. I had, for so long, been in an unfulfilling marriage, holding on to broken dreams and shattered hopes with seemingly no way out that I couldn't imagine having a better life. I agreed with the Lord that I had been marred, but there was no way I thought my life could possibly be transformed into something great and glorious. But I got the message. This moving ordeal was my Red Sea experience. I just had to wait. And wait I did. A little while later that same day, I received a phone call from a friend who had been a strong support throughout this entire ordeal. She was calling to tell me to come by her job to get the balance I needed for my security deposit. I was so very grateful!

While on my way there, another friend called to see how things were rolling along. I told her I was stranded with no one to help me move. She told me not to worry that God did not bring me this far to leave me. The help would come. By the time I made it back home, my friend called back to say she was on her way with another friend of hers to help me move. Two teachers who worked with me also came to help. Between our three cars and two SUV's we made two trips from Chicago to Lansing. None of the people who helped me move were relatives. All of them accept one had I known for only a little over a year. The other person I had never met in my life. In fact, I learned that he was not the kind of guy who liked moving. But he left his job downtown, went home in the far suburbs to change clothes, then drove to the city and loaded his car twice, just for us! Even now, when I think about how the Lord made a way for me that day, I'm still overwhelmed.

I have learned throughout my life that the people who you look to the most for help are not the ones who will necessarily be willing or available to help. As long as you continue to depend on others to rescue you, you will never experience the fulfillment of God's will for your life. Sometimes, your deliverance will make others uncomfortable; especially if you come out by any other way than by them or in a way that they can't comprehend. If I had waited on the people I thought would help me, I'd be still waiting today, and that's if I had remained alive.

PART III

LIKE A BUTTERFLY

"...unless a grain of wheat falls into the ground and dies, it remains alone; but if it dies, it produces much grain."
~ John 12:24

8

The butterfly is such a beautiful and natural illustration that God gave me to understand the changes that were taking place in my life. This marvelous creature has become my life's symbol.

The butterfly begins its life as a tiny egg that, because of its size, it's hard to see with the naked eye. At this stage of development, everything the butterfly is and will become is contained within that tiny egg. Even though the egg is so tiny and appears worthless and useless, there is so much energy and power on the inside that it *slowly*, but surely, manifests outward growth and development. During this most critical stage of development, if this egg is to survive the elements of nature, the butterfly that produces the egg, has to make sure it is placed in the safest environment possible. There are other insects that prey on the egg of the butterfly because that is where their nourishment comes from.

As it is with the butterfly, so it is with us. Here is when the elements of our environment can attack us to the point where our purpose can literally be destroyed beyond repair. There are people who thrive and survive on destroying your hopes and dreams. This is why it is imperative that you monitor who comes in and out of your life at any given time and how much of yourself you share with them. Some people will attach themselves to you and give the illusion that they are supporting you and "got your back," but, before you know it, they have stripped you of the very thing on which you had begun to build your hopes and dreams and made it their own.

From the egg of a butterfly comes a wingless, wormlike form called the larva. The very description suggests purposelessness and ugliness! But, during this stage, an even more significant form of development is taking place. The caterpillar forms and embarks upon a new life task, which is, to eat. What it eats at this stage causes it to grow and as it grows it sheds its skin. Destroying it at this phase in its development would hinder the caterpillar from fulfilling its total purpose. Sometimes, because of how ugly a thing looks, we tend to terminate it right away without giving it a chance to transform. Many times we fail to consider that our purpose must develop. The circumstances that we encounter along the way may not be pleasant or desirable, but this is part of the process.

9

Whatever your destiny and no matter how it looks or feels at this present moment, don't give up hope. Nourish it and feed it and it will grow! I cannot help but think about one of my nephews, who we nicknamed Biscuit (Duane, Jr.). He was born two months premature and needed to be in the special care nursery for the first few weeks of his life. The amazing thing about Biscuit is that he responded to all that was spoken into his life. We prayed for him, talked to him about his future, and let him know that his new bedroom was almost ready for him.

In less than one month after he was born, Biscuit was taken off all ventilators and medications to everyone's amazement. His next task, after being placed in the regular nursery, was to simply eat. At first, he could be fed only small amounts of baby formula per week. Then, because he began to show signs of steady progression, he was given more per day and eventually gained enough weight to go home.

What if everyone gave up on him because he was premature? What if no one spoke life into him? What if no one prayed for his full development? And, what if no one fed him? What my little nephew ate caused him to grow.

A caterpillar also grows because of what it eats. If it eats something poisonous, it will die. If it eats something beneficial to its development, it lives and continues to eat more! So it is with us. Whatever we feed our minds, bodies, and spirits is what we will grow into. Think about this for a moment. What kind of books do you read? Or, do you take the time to read? What kind of music do you listen to and why? With whom do you spend time socializing? Where do you go to relax and just have fun? What do you spend most of your time thinking about? What foods do you load up on? Chances are answering these questions will provide you with a blueprint of what your life is like right now. Ouch!

Are you happy with the results? Would you like to change what you have discovered? Then, change your "diet." And remember this, sometimes you may just have to dine alone.

Through much reading of leadership development and self-improvement materials, I have learned that it takes twenty-one days to develop a new habit. Make a list of changes you would like to make in each of the following areas: spiritual, intellectual, physical, emotional, economic, and social. Identify one thing you would like to change in each area. Develop a plan to read or engage in an activity that relates to each of your desired goals. Work toward something that's attainable but will provide you with enough of a challenge to keep you motivated. Now, here is the challenge: whatever you decide to do, commit to doing it for the next twenty-one days and see what happens in your life. Keeping a journal would be helpful. On the very last day, read through your journal and write down your final thoughts. This process has rescued me many times when I had lost focus of my vision. Going back and revisiting things I have written provides me with fuel to reignite the fire of motivation.

As the caterpillar continues to eat, it sheds its skin, or husk, as it grows. There's a vital message in this reality, one in which we fail to embrace at almost every turn in our lives. The bigger the caterpillar gets, it is literally forced out of its previous environment. Remember earlier when I mentioned that our environment has the ability to limit our growth? Well, I hope you can see it more clearly in this illustration. Imagine if the caterpillar refused to expand into its new environment, it would automatically have to stop eating in order to accommodate its limiting surroundings. If it stops eating, it stops growing. If it stops growing, it will meet an untimely death. This is what happens to us as we are trying to develop into our purpose. Sometimes fear, adverse circumstances, limited finances, family troubles, job issues, spiritual setbacks, and other situations begin to manifest. If we allow these things to stunt our growth, then what will become of God's purpose for our lives? What will become of all those who we were to impact with our gifts? If you are in an environment that seems to be hindering your growth, you must prayerfully assess your situation and make decisions based on the will of the Lord for your life.

Not all adversity is meant to stunt your growth. Sometimes, the adversity is what causes us to grow. The difference is how we approach it. The natural developmental process for a caterpillar at this point must be somewhat uncomfortable, but it embraces the opportunity to grow because innately, there is a greater purpose for it and this phase is necessary in order to obtain the greater outcome. A friend of mine would always encourage us by saying, "Our **not yet** is better than our **right now**"! You have to believe that! The word of the Lord confirms this in 1 John 3:2: "...and it has not yet been revealed what we shall be, but we know that when He is revealed, we shall be like Him, for we shall see Him as He is." I believe that whenever He appears in our situation, when He shows up in our circumstances, we shall be like Him! We **shall not** be the negative things that people and our circumstances dictate, but **we shall be like Him!** The caterpillar does not appear as it shall be before it is to become a butterfly. In fact, it looks nothing like a butterfly. But the essence of all that a butterfly entails is within it. And so it is in you! You don't look at all like what God has planned for you! We must remember that He created us in His image and after His likeness. His purpose for our lives is wrapped up in who He is, not in who we are or in who we appear to be at the present.

A caterpillar will always become a butterfly and nothing less! You **will** become **all** that God has ordained you to become and **nothing less!**

10

In its slimy and unattractive state, we find that the caterpillar's next stage of development is one that is easier on the eyes. It actually creates an environment for itself that hides the ugliness from all who would look upon it; it's the cocoon. Yes, that's right. When things get so bad and we just wish we could DISAPPEAR, the caterpillar does it better than we ever could. However, its reason for disappearing is purposeful to the development of its future. When the caterpillar begins to build a cocoon around itself, it is to position itself for its final phase of development. It must place itself in a resting position in order to experience a metamorphosis.

It is amazing that the material by which this cocoon is made is right on the inside of the caterpillar and is one of the finest in the world~ silk! Already, even in its ugliness, the caterpillar draws from something beautiful and valuable within itself to help it get to the next level! It is amazing that the Creator of the universe thought enough of the caterpillar to put within it something valuable to help it become what He designed it to be. How awesome is it to think about who you are and what He has put within you! Some individuals **desire** to hide because of feeling ugly, useless, and unimportant. Some individuals **need** to hide in order to be still before the Lord so they can identify that special thing inside of them and use it to get to their next level. It is the *purpose* and *work* behind the hiding that will determine our destiny! Up until the point of building a cocoon, the caterpillar has completed all that it can on its own, as far as his developmental process is concerned.

The final stage rests with the timing of the Creator's will. In my study of the butterfly, I learned that while in the cocoon, the caterpillar begins to form new cells, which causes the old ones to dissolve, thus forming a new creature—the butterfly. This sounds a lot like 2 Corinthians 5:17: "Therefore, if anyone is in Christ, he is a new creation; old things have passed away; behold, all things have become new."

Before the butterfly can exit the cocoon, it has to vigorously rub its wings together to build up the blood vessels in its wings. If this process is interrupted, say by human hands assisting with the breaking forth from the cocoon, the butterfly will die. It needs to struggle inside the cocoon in order to build strength in its wings so that it can break forth on its own at the appointed time and take flight. However, before taking flight, it spreads its wings, which act as solar panels and soak up the sun. The energy from the sun gives it the power it needs to actually take flight.

PART IV

MARRED & MANGLED, BUT MAKING IT

"And the vessel that he made of clay was marred in the hand of the potter; so he made it again into another vessel, as it seemed good to the potter to make."
~Jeremiah 18:4

11

The lessons of the butterfly are what the Lord used during this time to teach me how to embrace His will for my life. My sons and I experienced many hardships that was meant to destroy us. We were marred and mangled, but making it. In other words, we experienced emotional wounds and hurts from the brokenness of what our family once represented, but we were determined to continue moving forward and not to look back. Life as we once knew it was over and a wide open future lay ahead. Our only consolation at this point was that we knew God would never leave us and that He was truly our covering and provider.

Once the boys and I were moved into the new apartment, it was time to regroup and move forward. But I had no clue what my next steps were to be. I spent most of my time living in a fog. I had heard people say that fog means the "favor of God." If that's the case, then I would definitely have to agree. There was no way I could have made it without His favor or without the lessons I learned from the butterfly.

When we moved, we had no furniture. All we took were our clothes, books, toys, some of the children's games, and a few dishes and cookware. I sat on the floor of the apartment one day while the boys took a nap and just cried. How and where will I get beds for the boys? I didn't mind sleeping on the floor, but I did not want my boys sleeping on the floor. I had already purchased them a bed, but I left it behind so that they would have a place to sleep whenever they went with their Dad. Well, later that evening while the boys and I were running errands, a friend of mine called to say that at that very moment beds were being purchased for the boys and my address was needed for delivery. I could not believe it! The Lord had touched the heart of one of their mentors, and later that week they were surprised with a bunk bed set and a twin bed for my oldest son. All glory to God! The boys were beginning to see the hand of God at work in our lives!

Wouldn't you know that with every blessing, there seemed to be a major setback for us? One week after moving in and the boys being blessed with their beds, I lost my car. Fortunately I had just started my vacation, so I didn't need a car right away. A friend of mine, Sheila, offered to teach me how to drive her Honda, which had a stick shift. That was quite an experience but a much needed blessing.

By the time school started in the autumn, the transmission on the Honda went out. However, my supervisor was selling her grandmother's Mercury Sable and asked me if I knew anyone looking to buy a car. Of course! *I was,* even though I didn't have the money at the time, putting me at risk of missing out on this opportunity. So I prayed for God to move in the situation, and He did. Without me having to ask, a friend who heard of my ordeal offered to provide me with the funds to purchase the car if I agreed to a ridiculously low interest loan with minimal payments. I agreed. My prayer then was to pay the loan back ahead of time, which I was able to do. Glory to God!

With mounting financial pressures, I was unable to consistently balance a budget. No matter what budget plan I created, the funds would not cooperate. This was disappointing to me because financial astuteness has been a lifelong goal of mine. I had read all the latest information regarding investing and had even taken advantage of an entrepreneurial opportunity to educate others on the basic principles of financial literacy after having learned them myself. My desire was and still is to position myself and my sons to earn most of our income as business owners and investors. While being coached through Robert Kiyosaki's financial program, I obtained his board game, which teaches financial literacy and the principles of investing. The boys and I would play this game for hours and then have deep discussions on what we needed to do to make the game our reality.

I struggled constantly with having to decide whether to pay the light bill or buy groceries; if I split it in half, will I have enough to spare for laundry? Rent increases ate up any salary increases I earned. On top of all this, during that first year, I was in the middle of divorce proceedings and graduate school and was juggling three positions on my job due to staff transitions all while trying to stay on top of four boys in two new schools. I had little room to breathe. I buried myself in my work and the Word of God and prayer. I knew from what the Lord had taught me about the butterfly that, as uncomfortable as this was, there was strength to be gained in my struggle.

12

My sons were awesome during this entire ordeal. Their home training began to manifest. Based on society's statistics, where I thought I would experience failing grades, delinquent behavior, and rebellious attitudes, I witnessed the opposite. That's not to say I didn't have to chastise them and make phone calls for assistance from a mentor or two from time to time, but I knew I was experiencing something unique in their upbringing. I thought back to each time I discovered I was expecting, I would anoint my stomach with oil and pray a prayer of health, safety, and obedience over each one of my sons. I knew that no matter what happened in life, if they had an obedient spirit, they would eat the good of the land (Isaiah 1:19).

It was during this time of transition that their musical gifts began to flourish. A year before we moved, B.J had come to me and said, "Momma, I'm not supposed to tell you, so don't say anything, but Daddy put me in drum lessons in Indiana with a man named Butch McGee." Well, although this news was quite shocking to me, I informed my son that that was a good thing his father was doing for him and there was nothing for him to feel guilty about. I thanked him for being honest with me and let him know that he had my 100% support.

B.J, since the age of about two, expressed an interest in music. I first noticed it when I heard nursery rhymes being played on a little piano we bought him for Christmas. Since songs had been programmed into the piano, I just assumed that that's what I was listening to until I stood in his doorway and watched him tap out the songs himself. I was awestruck! Shortly thereafter, he took a **strong** liking to playing the drums. At three years old, when it was time for us to go home from a family holiday dinner, B.J refused to relinquish the drum set one of his uncles had in his home. He wanted to remain seated with sticks in hand, very carefully focusing on which drums to hit next. Unlike most little boys his age, he did not bang on the drums; he actually "played" them.

B.J. expressed an interest in joining the Junior High School band at the new school. Although this was a new experience for us, I felt the Lord's blessing on it. It would mean sacrificing more time and money, but I knew this was B.J's gift and wanted him to excel in it. By the end of the school year, when it was time for him to graduate, he received many honors and awards, both academically and musically. The school's band director was very impressed with his skills and maturity, especially since this was his first experience playing in a school band. His enthusiasm and success with the band paved the way for his brothers to join him later.

Nicholas was drawn to the bass guitar and taught himself how to play at the age of 10. I still remember how reluctant he was when his older brother recommended that he join the high school band as the new bass player, replacing the former one who had graduated. It took quite an entourage of his peers to coerce him, but he finally gave in and did extremely well. His band director told the story of how he gave Nick lessons for three weeks then turned him loose and watched him master any piece of music that was placed before him. Nicholas, too, received not only high academic honor awards but some of the top musicianship awards also upon graduating high school.

Justin and Caleb were not far behind in their musical gifts. Justin loved watching Byron play the drums and desired to learn as well. As soon as he was old enough, Justin also began taking drum lessons with the famed Butch McGee. Justin always had a distinct style all his own to whatever he did and playing the drums was no exception. He not only had to have the skill but also had to exhibit the aura of a gifted drummer was also important. Justin seemed to always approach his craft with the utmost seriousness. He would be found often studying and practicing what he deemed the best techniques from other artists using video postings on YouTube.

Caleb was the one who really surprised me with his musical ability because he seemed to be interested in only cars and computers, proving himself to be technologically savvy. Being the youngest, Caleb had never seemed intimidated by his brothers' talents. At birth, being the biggest of all the boys, he weighed in at 8 lbs. 4 oz. His fat cheeks earned him the nickname of Dizzy Gillespie, even though it turned out that Caleb was a natural on the baritone (miniature tuba) not the trumpet like Gillespie. During auditions in middle-school, he scored extremely high on the baritone. But being a natural did present its challenges: he despised practicing. His private lessons teacher was often frustrated with him because he was very talented but didn't take playing the instrument seriously. Other students would labor in practice and barely be able to play and Caleb would spend as less time as possible and play effortlessly when it was time to perform.

Caleb shocked all of us when he played a solo piece at the middle school's winter concert his first year. He had not told us he was going to be featured, so we all held our breath when he began to play. He did extremely well! His brothers looked on in disbelief, wondering when Caleb had actually practiced. Once he reached high school, Caleb thought he'd try his hand at other instruments, but none displayed his talent as well as the baritone. When he played with his brother's at church, he played the congas since he didn't have a baritone of his own. Playing at church allowed all of them to develop and regularly use their gifts.

The Pickett Boys, as they are affectionately called, never cease to amaze me. As a mother of all sons, I spent a lot of time in prayer. There is so much going on in society today, especially with young African American men, that your heart can become overcome with fear. Instead of accepting the status quo for my sons, I decided to set the standard for them. I was determined to provide them with as much knowledge and wisdom as possible to prepare them for life beyond my doors.

One thing I had never done was tell them I was going to do something and did not do it. It didn't matter if it was a reward or consequence. If I said I was going to do it, I did it. I also made it my business to apologize to my sons if I had made a mistake. Of course, they were diligent in pointing out these occasions, but they are permitted to do so.

My relationship with them was never about control; I taught discipline. If you made a mistake, learn the lesson and hold *yourself* accountable for what you have learned is what I taught. I lived my life by this principle and modeled it before them daily.

Ever since the boys were big enough to hold something in their hand and walk without falling, they were responsible for cleaning up their own toys and clothes. With advancement in age, they had increases in their responsibilities. There was no way I was going to cook, clean, wash, and work a full-time job with all those muscles and energy in my home. Keeping my children preoccupied with responsibilities increased their physical and mental growth and development, and they have been found to be too exhausted to participate in idle activities whether day or night.

With all that the boys and I had experienced, I did not have the energy or the time to be a private investigator for four charges. They grew up respecting me and each other. Yes, I corrected some behaviors, but this was part of their learning. They were brought up to understand that cleanliness is godliness. I taught them *how* to wash themselves. I kept their hair cut and lined (until I turned 40 and they made me promise not to cut their hair ever again). I did not allow them to walk around dressed like thugs: they represented God, their parents, and themselves. I went so far as to tell them that if they wanted to dress like thugs, I would dress like the women who hung around the thugs. Since they were dead set against that, we were pretty much in agreement concerning the dress code.

I continued to pray God's blessings on their lives as they grew and developed into the men God was designing them to be, but I also encouraged them to establish their own personal relationship with the Lord through prayer, fasting, and Bible study.

13

𝓔ven though the boys and I were starting to settle down in our new apartment, the challenges continued to surface. I remembered the summer when I was unable to pay a mounting electric bill and our service was disconnected for 40 days. Of course everything in our apartment operated by electricity, so you can imagine what a struggle this was. There were only a few people who knew that our electricity had been turned off. As some expressed, since I was working, I'd have it back on in a jiffy. Oh how wrong they were!

The day the electricity was turned off was the first day of the summer camp program at my job and the boy's triathlon camp. We learned quite a few survival skills during this time, some of which were keeping necessary food items in a cooler and making it home to take quick, but thorough showers by way of candle light and cold water before it got too dark at night. As far as clothing was concerned, wash and wear items from our wardrobe was the fashion of the day. By the time we got settled in after all this, it was bedtime. At one point, just to keep my sanity, I told them we could act as if we were on a camping trip or we could pretend to be in the army, out in the fields. Thank God for boys! I was grateful that we lived on the fourth floor of our building because we could keep all the windows and our patio door opened during the summer nights without worrying that someone would come in on us. The boys and I also prayed fervently that the Lord would keep the temperatures cool at night just so we could endure. He answered that prayer for us pretty much the entire time.

In order for service to be restored, I had to pay the entire bill. This was a challenge for me because my funds were extremely tight; so I continued to juggle the funds and pray for an answer to the problem. I did seek assistance from ComEd through CEDA (Community Economic Development Association), but wouldn't you know it? It would take 30 days for them to get the funds to me. While waiting for the money, I discovered that my account number had been incorrectly entered in the system, so the assistance was never generated for me. Oh the frustration of it all! I grew up believing that *faith without works is dead,* but it seemed as if all the work I was doing to support my faith was in vain, garnering no positive results. But through this situation I learned to never stop hoping for a miracle. I knew that somehow and some way God would show.

Leading up to the last day of the summer camp programs, while in a conversation with a friend I confided in him about the gravity of our situation. No one knew we had been living without electricity that long; no one could tell. I never missed work and the boys never missed camp. We remained clean, good-looking, and upbeat. Needless to say, on the way home from camp that Friday, I was able to tell the boys that we had help with the bill and the lights would be on by Monday. As we walked through the door of our apartment, Nicholas flicked the switch and the lights came on! "I knew it!" he shouted. His prayer was that we would not have to wait until Monday, but that the lights would be on when we got home. We all began jumping around and praising the Lord because He had once again met a need in a miraculous way!

14

Remaining faithful to the Lord during these trying times was the only option. I knew that if I was going to come out victoriously, I had to keep God first in my life. I was also determined to use every experience as teachable moments for all of us. This mindset caused me to shun any opportunities for selfish pleasures that would interfere with God's handiwork in our lives and the sound development of my sons' overall growth as young men. Besides, I'd seen enough in my life of what happened to other women who decided to "help God out," and I had no desire to travel down that road. So I took the road less traveled. This does not mean that tempting opportunities did not present themselves. Just the opposite happened.

A plethora of social, financial, and relational opportunities bombarded me, usually at times when I was the most vulnerable. Thank God for the Holy Spirit; He's truly able to keep us from falling and being knocked out cold in the process. So, continuing to bury myself in my work, rearing my children, and working in the ministry at my local church became my steadfast mode of operation. In fact, my daily prayer was one of being settled and established in life. The boys were growing up too fast, and soon I would be facing the reality of having an empty nest.

I needed to focus on preparing myself financially in order to be able to face my future. I had always wanted to start a couple of businesses centered on my creative gifts and was looking forward to expanding these options on a part time basis while still working 9 to 5. I had already created a mentoring program for young people and had written the curriculum to support it. With the encouragement of my family, I started tampering with the idea of starting a cookie business, which appeared to want to take off without me. I had to put the brakes on it on several occasions until I was mentally and physically ready to launch it. My life seemed to be moving right along. I was still juggling financial issues, but I felt hopeful that implementing a business plan would allow me the opportunity to generate more income to finally begin ridding us of our debts. Besides, the boys could help build the businesses and assist with the operations, thereby solidifying the skills we all learned from playing Robert Kiyosaki's Cash Flow game. I continued seeking direction for my life, as I felt the winds of change blowing.

The first wind swirled in the work place. I was offered an opportunity with a different agency. This happened at the perfect time because my departure allowed for one of my colleagues to not be displaced. She was able to keep her position, and I was able to move forward in my career as an after school program manager.

At my new school site with the new agency, I looked forward to new challenges. There were many patiently waiting for me at my door on my first day. Each challenge was met with a sense of energy and excitement, and it didn't take long for me to establish an organized plan of action to meet the needs of this new school. Things were really starting to look up, that is, until the second wind blew, and I fell down...literally!

It happened on Thursday, May 6, 2010, at around 5:15 p.m. I don't think I'll ever forget that day, seeing that it is right up there with all the other major life-transforming events.

After conducting a parent-training meeting, I climbed three flights of stairs to my third floor office with an armload of binders and other supplies. Upon reaching the top, I took a few steps and ended up on the floor. It took a few seconds for me to realize what happened, as I looked at all my materials scattered across the floor and yelled out to whomever could hear me that I had fallen. That's when I noticed that the shininess of the floor was really water from a fresh mopping by the custodian.

Thus began the event that triggered what I came to call the beginning of the end of my life as I knew it. My life was about to change in a way that I could never have imagined.

PART V

To Never Give Up!

"Being confident of this very thing, that He who has begun a good work in you will complete it until the day of Jesus Christ."
~Philippians 1:6

15

Sometimes, while going through hard trials and tests for an extended period of time, I felt invisible to the world around me. The feeling that no one knew, cared, or could help me out of my stuck place always seemed to loom over my head. This is where fear and frustration often tried to gain control and send me into a tailspin of implosive emotions and actions. Here is where I learned a very important lesson about the use of *struggle* in fulfilling God's purpose in my life as I experienced a certain "death" occurrence beginning to take shape in my life. I like to call it "*death by destiny.*"

When something dies it no longer remains. It no longer responds because it simply cannot. Because it is dead, its purpose is no longer the same. Dead things usually end up being hidden away beneath the earth. Dead things have a purpose, too, though, and, that is, to usher in new life. Jesus once revealed to his disciples that "...unless a grain of wheat falls into the ground and dies, it remains alone; but if it dies, it produces much grain" (John 12:24). No one, with the natural eye, observes the actual growth process of a grain of wheat when it falls into the ground and dies. Some may see it fall and come to the conclusion that life is over for that seed. But there is a greater purpose for the death!

The rich soil and the nutrients in the natural hidden environment regenerate that dying seed, causing it to bring forth new life. It's the new life that amazes everyone who witnessed the initial death of the seed. It's not what's on the outside that sustains a person; it's what lies on the inside. Like the caterpillar, I learned to reach down inside of myself and use what's been put there to create a new life for my sons and me. My "death" came by way of the injury I sustained on the job.

Why, at a time when I knew I had overcome the worst struggles, did I now have to actually endure physical pain as well? As this experience lingered, the financial struggles, emotional hurts, and mental stresses became greater. Like Job, the thing I feared the most had come upon me. While undergoing physical therapy for the injured shoulder, I was terminated from my job. Initially, I experienced a frozen, fearful sensation running down my spine and gripping my heart. The boys and I had been through so much already; *when would all this end*?! One of my favorite scriptures is Psalm 138:8, which says, *"The Lord will perfect that which concerns me; Your mercy, O Lord, endures forever; Do not forsake the works of Your hands."* This I kept reading and repeating to myself daily.

I was now stuck living without one-third of my salary until I was released from doctor's care. I didn't know how long this would last, so, once again, I had to make major adjustments in order to survive, only this time I was dealing with constant physical pain. Just because I was injured didn't mean the rest of my life was on hold. I continued to deal with the obligations of being a mother and head of household. Here I was, after deciding early on that I would not become a statistic, becoming one anyway. I cannot describe the emotional pain I endured during this time. It was quite different from earlier in my life.

When you are known as a hardworking, organized, focused, intelligent, and God-fearing individual who can handle difficult situations with great faith, it's very difficult to accept and explain to others the indigent predicament in which you may find yourself. There were many family members and friends, who like Job's friends, could not understand my state. Some thought I was exaggerating my circumstances because the boys and I never appeared to be in distress. Some expressed that I just wanted to be bailed out from financial pressure. Others were afraid to get involved. Some concluded that I had sinned and this was my judgment. Some, sad to say, waited to see when I would have a nervous breakdown or have some other attack that would take me out.

Just trying to find a trustworthy someone who would be a strong support for me and the boys became another pressure point for me. Being a private person, sharing my troubles and risking having someone else make light of them or use the information for their advantage or even use it against me were major concerns. Thank God for sending the right people at the right time to be that support for us. I felt I needed to protect my children in all this as well and didn't want them negatively impacted.

Whenever I felt that my supporters were becoming overbearing and not providing direction according to the will of God, I would quietly pull away. I needed to know that God was in control at every moment and not someone else. My way of enduring publicly was to grin and bear it. There were some who had no idea with what I was dealing. When things seemed the worse and I had no energy or will to move forward, the Holy Spirit would give me a song. The words would penetrate my spirit repetitively, and like a spiritual IV, it would fill me with hope and life.

I constantly faced the possibility of losing my possessions and just losing *"it"*. I suffered severe panic attacks while at home, while driving, and even while visiting my mother in the hospital. And the troubles kept mounting: just as winter was ending, I lost my apartment. We remained homeless for quite some time. I ended up driving between two suburbs and the city until we found temporary housing where we could all, once again, be together in one place. And then, my car was repossessed the Friday before Mother's Day. In addition to this, I was facing two graduations in the late spring I felt as though I was running out of steam.

We prayed for the Lord to make a way for us and He did. I was able to rent a car for that weekend and retrieve my car by the middle of the following week.

16

But in the middle of all these hardships, God remained faithful. Through an event hosted by the Illinois Secretary of State, for which I was asked to prepare cookies, I was blessed to be introduced to Otis Wilson, a former Chicago Bear and NFL Super Bowl champion, who was on a quest of finding someone to develop a literacy program for his foundation. God was manifesting His purpose for my life in the midst of my pain. The opportunity of this project caused me to remember that God still had a plan for my life and gave me the strength I needed to keep fighting and pressing forward despite being homeless and destitute.

As the literacy project began to wind down, so did my car, which needed $1,500 worth of work. I needed yet another miracle. I couldn't afford it: I was still scuffling to pay the car note and other bills as well, all while still not working. Once again, God touched the heart of my god brother, who kept the car in fair running condition until I could get it fixed.

Although our state of destitution threatened to immobilize us, we were able to continue functioning with courage, grace, and dignity. We made it through both graduations and my oldest son's decision to attend Berklee College of Music in the fall. I sought diligently, but unsuccessfully, for work for several months. I continued to trust and lean on the Lord although I felt myself giving out.

There were many nights I cried and prayed for relief. This often led me to begin praying for others who may have been going through as I was or even worse. Interceding for someone else gave me hope that God was meeting their need and gave me strength to go forward. And, then, I was hit—literally!

On June 17, 2011, while waiting at a stoplight to make a right turn, I was hit from behind, causing me to hit the truck in front of me. I was knocked unconscious, my driver's seat was dislocated, and a strapped, wedge-heeled sandal was knocked off my foot. While my 2006 Ford Taurus was totaled, I miraculously sustained no life-threatening injuries; I had only a concussion and bruised knees and legs and had to endure physical pain for quite some time. A month later, I begin to suffer from post-traumatic stress and post-concussion syndromes, which lasted some four months. Anxiety attacks, heart palpitations, and feelings of extreme fear and dread were just some of the challenges I periodically dealt with without warning.

The weight of it all became unbearable. It was as if my entire life was caving in on me. Eighteen years of struggling beyond belief had taken its toll, and I had no more fight left in me. That's why, on the morning after I failed to remember to recertify for unemployment benefits, I decided enough was enough. I struggled to see beyond the years of pain, suffering, rejection, loneliness, and the constant struggle to survive. I had escaped physically but was stuck mentally, emotionally, spiritually, and economically.

At this point, ***I gave up to Christ*** in a way that I never had before. I had nothing left and let Him know that it was all on Him to get me through or take me out. My hope in Christ is what got me through this very dark time and gave me the courage to never give up!

17

Once we make a conscious decision and effort to surrender to the Lord, He is more than ready, willing, and able to move on our behalf. Many times we get angry with others for not stepping in and making things better when we get into a jam, but this has never been the will of God for us. He wants us to totally *trust Him* for every solution to our challenges. He wants us to *trust Him* to select the individuals to assist us. He wants us to *trust Him* to make the connections for us to get that new job, new home, or spouse.

I have always been blown away at how the Lord made connections in my life and brought people into my life to, not only help me through a challenge, but also speak life and purpose into me. Their lives were a reflection of God's power and glory and this generated life into me because I continuously sought God's presence.

Writing this book was the means to launch me into the new life Christ prepared for me from the beginning of time. I had actually completed the book five years ago. Every time I would attempt to get it published, something would always prevent me. I was beginning to feel like a hypocrite to those who knew of my intentions.

Two weeks before I decided to just give up, I kept hearing the Spirit telling me to write. My response was, *"Write what?!"* I had already written a book that I couldn't seem to get published, so in my finite mind I wondered why should I start something else.

If it sounds like I had an attitude, I did! However, in order to not offend the Spirit, I repented and just begin writing in my journal. After all, I *was* writing. I kept feeling a nudge to go back to the same book and insert personal examples of how I overcame the struggles in my life. I ignored this nudging because I didn't want others to know my business. I didn't want to be embarrassed or to embarrass anyone else. I was allowing pride to keep me in bondage.

One of the very great things about the Lord that I truly admire is that He never gives up on us. He knew the only way to get me to move in the right direction was through His spirit moving in someone I would never expect. Early on, I mentioned that as a young girl, I would have visions of myself as an adult speaking to many people. I kept this to myself because I couldn't understand it. Well, on the morning I decided to give up, my sons' mentor, Dwayne Bryant, called me with a similar vision that left me close to speechless. No one, outside of myself, had ever had that clear of a vision of my life. It was similar to what I had seen as a child, but magnified exponentially! The Lord had to bring out special reinforcements to get me to move in His will. He knew who to use and when to use them. I knew it was time for me to get to work. Besides, I wanted to see how He would use this to reconstruct my broken life.

Not soon after I was given the assignment from the Lord to write, I begin experiencing an increase in the post-concussion symptoms. Prior to this, my symptoms had actually begun to decrease. Anxiety attacks surfaced daily, anytime and anywhere—while driving, while in the library, while at the store, and even in church. Then, the bouts of insomnia began. This was something I had never experienced before. I would lie down and shortly after dozing off to sleep, I would wake up with such a feeling of dread that I cannot adequately describe it even to this day. My eyes would be so heavy I could hardly keep them open, but I just could not fall asleep. I would pray and read the Bible and fall off to sleep. Then, within minutes, the cycle would repeat itself all over again.

One condition seemed to feed the next. I continued to fight through it. I refused to take medication because I was not willing to accept what I knew was an attack from the enemy. I recognized this for what it really was, just another test of struggle coming my way. This only signaled that a life change was imminent.

Sometimes, the change we're expecting is not all about us. I never dismissed the fact that my sons were a part of this struggle and, therefore, had concerns of their own. As much as dwelt in me, I tried my best to make sure the lines of communication remained open between us. I listened to what ailed them and prayed with them for their personal strength and determination to the right things. Through all of what we were experiencing, they were learning to trust God for themselves. One such instance brought about a life-changing experience for my oldest son, Byron.

18

The success my sons experienced in school did not come easy. So, of course, every success was met with a great deal of joy on my part. In 2011, in the middle of dealing with so many challenges, I also had two graduations to celebrate. My youngest son was transitioning from middle-school to high school and my oldest from high school to college. Byron had received a full-tuition scholarship from Berklee College of Music in Boston, Massachusetts. We were more than thrilled and grateful to the Lord for this great blessing! He was to begin school on September 4th. We discovered that with all the financial aid he received he still needed a significant amount of money to cover room and board and other school fees. Because I was not working and had no other support to fill in the gap, B.J was unable to begin school in the fall. I was heartbroken and devastated, and so was B.J. The amazing thing was he didn't allow this setback to get him down. He continued assisting with the high school band while he worked diligently in seeking more scholarships and grants to cover the shortfall. I often could see the hurt, frustration, confusion, and feel his embarrassment as he struggled with not being able to go to school after having worked so hard and having accomplished so much. I did the only thing I could do and knew how to do: I cried out to God. B.J also spent time in prayer, seeking God for help. He never allowed bitterness or anger to creep in his heart. As the months rolled on, the sense of urgency escalated.

I believe the Lord used Mother Martha Bryant to plant another seed of "never giving up" in me during this time. Everything that happened after she strongly encouraged me to not allow Byron to lose his scholarship money no matter what fueled my courage to fight harder. It's nothing but appropriate that Mother Martha, someone I esteem and trust as a mentor, is the mother of the boy's mentor. If in no other case than this one, it's true that the apple doesn't fall far from the tree. "As iron sharpens iron, So a man sharpens the countenance of his friend" (Proverbs 27:17). A series of events happening in quick succession brought about a miracle!

Byron and the band he and his friends and brothers formed were asked to provide entertainment at an art show one Sunday evening in December. Since the event was not far from their mentor, they invited him to come hear them perform. Midway through the event, Dwayne arrived and was excited about the band and how the boys had grown up. He asked me what was happening with Byron getting off to school. I told him so far nothing had changed and that I didn't know what else to do. He showed me a message he was sending to some of his contacts regarding Byron and then looked at me and said, "Woman, you need to write the newspaper about him. People would love to help a kid like him." Before I could ask which newspaper, the name Mary Mitchell came to me. I had never met her but had read some of her articles over the years. I told Dwayne that I would write her the very next day and keep him posted.

Early that Monday morning, after my prayer time, I begin to write the letter. I cast away my shame and embarrassment over my struggles and wrote to Mary Mitchell of the Chicago Sun-Times about Byron's dilemma. All while I wrote, I prayed and cried. I knew this was my last and best effort to help my son. Once the letter was finished, we prayed over it and mailed it. On Friday morning, I received a phone call from Mary informing me that she received my letter and was compelled to do the story! She gathered more information about us and requested a reference that could validate all I shared with her. Of the two individuals I referred, she chose Dwayne, seeing that he had known us longer and had already made tangible investments in the boys' lives. Mary informed me that the article would be in that Sunday's (December 18th) newspaper. I was excited, nervous, ambivalent, and downright scared! I didn't know what was going to happen; and the more I thought about the number of people who would read the article and how many of those people knew us personally, my feelings and emotions grew. I could sense that Byron was just as nervous. His brothers, on the other hand, were much more optimistic. They were looking for instant celebrity status. Would this really help us or would it hurt us even more? There was nothing to do but wait.

By Sunday, things began to unfold like wildfire. Just as I was leaving church, Nicholas texted me to say one of his schoolmates saw the article in the paper. I went to pick up a couple of copies as soon as I left church. I was so nervous. I sat in my truck and read the article as tears welled up in my eyes. I couldn't believe I was reading about our lives in the Sunday newspaper! I texted Dwayne to let him know the article was in the paper. I tried reading the article from an objective point of view but ended up crying even more. If this was anyone else besides me and my son, I would do whatever I could to help. I thanked God for giving me the strength to move in this direction but asked Him to keep His hand on it to make it good. He did!

By Monday morning, word had begun to spread. Family members and friends begin calling about the article. Byron and I contacted Mary again to thank her for choosing our story. What I didn't know was that a television morning news show had also shared the story on the air. I actually found that out when I went for a doctor's appointment and the office staff congratulated me when I walked through the door. I was amazed! I couldn't wait to tell Byron. He was excited and nervous as much as I was. I continued to believe God for the unfolding miracle.

On Wednesday afternoon, we received another phone call from Mary. She wanted to give us an update on how the public was responding to our story. Byron and I were quite surprised to discover that half of what he needed had already been sent in to Mary's office and more was still coming! I cried and Byron looked shocked! We thanked her profusely. She wanted us to know that she was going to place an article in Thursday's paper to update the public on the progress that was being made for Byron.

By Monday of the following week, Mary contacted us again saying we needed to schedule a time to meet to wrap this up or people would never stop sending money. All gifts received were made payable directly to Berklee College of Music and would be deposited right in Byron's account at the school. We made plans to meet on Wednesday morning at Dwayne's home. Byron and I talked about the wonderful thing that was unfolding before our eyes, but we knew we were not out of the woods yet. Even though it appeared that he would have the funds needed to attend school, we didn't have the means to ship his belongings or for airfare and hotel to get to Boston. Our resolve was to leave this in God's hands, too.

As we arrived at Dwayne's home on that Wednesday morning, we really had no clue as to what was about to unfold. My stomach felt queasy and I felt as if I were running on autopilot. I know Byron was more excited than nervous and couldn't wait to hear the outcome. For the first time since this entire matter unfolded, we were finally able to meet Mary face to face. From that day to this one, I call her my Christmas Angel. It was a challenge for me not to break down and cry torrents in front of everyone while expressing my utmost gratitude for everything that had been done to help my son. Dwayne made breakfast for everyone, but I couldn't eat. Water was the best I could do. After the formal introductions and small talk were over, it was time for the BIG REVEAL. Dwayne had a videographer there to record the entire event and a Sun-Times photographer accompanied Mary to capture pictures for the newspaper. This was all surreal for me as someone who prefers to stay in the background and who is definitely camera shy. I didn't have a chance to think about if my hair looked okay or how I sounded because the entire event unfolded so smoothly. I concentrated on not breaking down in tears during the interview.

Mary began by recapping the initial request I made via the letter and the public's immediate response in the following days. She poured over 200 letters all over a coffee table in front of us so we could actually see the kindness strangers displayed in meeting Byron's need to fulfill his dream. Mary read a few of the letters with us revealing that not all donors were wealthy individuals with stockpiles of funds to give away. These were individuals who were on fixed incomes, experiencing financial difficulties, and experiencing challenges with their own children; there were even responses from children who gave money that would have gone toward a Christmas present for themselves. Some of the letters were from other states. They all saw hope in Byron. This touched my heart in such a deep way; I cannot to this day fully put it into words.

Mary revealed that more than $18,000 had been given by the public to more than cover the shortfall Byron needed to get to school! Not only that, but a local UPS company owned by a mother and son, Barbara and Ray Weary, committed to making sure his things would be shipped to and from Berklee every year he was in school FOR FREE! I could not have paid for the smile that grew on Byron's face at that moment! I felt his joy, his burden lift, and his hope restored! For a mother, this is something indescribable! To know that what you have instilled in your child has produced the desired results and to see it being challenged by life's circumstances and then overcome by the hand of God is powerful to behold! What we came to discover next was that the blessings did not stop there.

Dwayne asked Byron how he was going to get to school now that he knew he would be able to go. Byron looked at me and both of us nervously laughed thinking of my poorly running truck. Dwayne made light of my truck for a few minutes, all in good jest because he knew what was to come. After his jovial antics, he presented us with airlines tickets to (and from, for me) to Boston along with hotel reservations to cover the time I would need to be in Boston and then some. This is when I could not hold back the tears. This was more than I expected or ever dreamed would happen for us. At this moment, it was Byron who felt my joy, my burden lift, and my hope restored! What an unbelievable blessing!

Dwayne then introduced Byron to someone who would step in as another mentor to him; Derrick Young, the traffic reporter for our local Channel Two news station, had been touched by Byron's diligence also. He presented Byron with a $100 gift card and a commitment to be available for Byron anytime during the course of his college career. Another stable source of strength and a listening ear was definitely welcomed. What more can I say? Among all other necessities, Byron packed up some of the letters that were sent to him by gracious donors in order to keep him motivated during tough times while at school.

By spring break, he was ready for a break from school and looking forward to coming home for a breather. Everyone was excited to see him and hear how the first part of his semester went for him. I was proud to see how much Byron had matured. By the end of his first semester at Berklee, Byron achieved straight A's with a grade point average of 3.96! He was so excited when his grades came that he immediately contacted Mary, Dwayne, and all his Facebook friends to let them know how well he had done. All congratulated him and Mary provided the public with the update in an article she wrote in the Chicago Sun-Times on May 31, 2012. The surprising backstory to all this, as was told at Byron's thank-you concert to the public by Mary, is that she was advised by a colleague to disregard my letter because it was a scam! But Mary felt compelled to not follow her colleague's advice and made the decision to publish our story. To God be all the glory!!!

As I'm ending this chapter, my heart is full of praise because of all that God continues to do for us. Not only has Byron returned to Berklee to continue fulfilling his dream and God's will for his life, but Nicholas, who also received scholarships covering his full tuition along with enough financial aid to cover all expenses, is attending the University of Illinois at Urbana-Champaign. Justin is on his way to Illinois State University this fall and Caleb will be completing his final year of high school this upcoming school year. My God is awesome!

19

Struggle is not a word that is favorable to many of us. As a matter of fact, if we could avoid struggle, we would feel a lot better about living. However, the best things and the most necessary things in life all involve a process involving struggle.

According to Webster's New Explorer Dictionary and Thesaurus, *struggle* means to "make strenuous efforts against opposition: strive; to proceed with difficulty or with great effort." My story has been one of struggle. However, I have come to realize that the best things in life are gotten by struggle. With all that I have gone through and even knowing that as I write this I'm not out of the woods as of yet, I know I am one of the most blessed women on the face of the planet! With so much lost, I have gained so much more. When I think of all the vacations, shopping sprees, personal spa times, luxury goods, a romantic relationship, and fancy dining experiences I had to forego in order to establish a solid foundation for my children and build our lives on the principles of the Word of God, only to allow His glory to shine through our lives, I smile.

We need to be the living examples and testimonies of the Lord's faithfulness in the earth. I really desire to encourage you to not be afraid of fulfilling your purpose in life. Don't be afraid of the struggle needed to get to the powerful part of your life. Never give up on yourself. Never give up on God! Be courageous! Courage denotes having a mindset that allows you to face difficulty, danger, and pain *without fear*. People need you to fulfill your purpose because they are attached to you in the Spirit. You may very well be the springboard for someone else's launch or flight.

My reason for penning this work is to encourage you to never give up in your search for purpose but to ***stand***, knowing that what the Lord has planned to do in your life, He will DO IT! I have found that the key for us is to remain "steadfast, unmovable, always abounding in the work of the Lord... (1 Corinthians 15:58).

Someone once said: begin to be now what you will be hereafter! Know that having a purpose in life is universal to everyone's existence. Understand that knowing your purpose and fulfilling your purpose are two separate factors you need in order to live a powerful life. Realize that the process for emerging from the *knowing* to the *fulfilling* of your purpose involves *struggle*! Be encouraged and embrace the fact that struggle is necessary for your transformation. A caterpillar transforms into a butterfly by surrendering to the Creator's original design for its life. No matter which phase of the process it endures, it Never Gives Up. Neither should you!

www.ingramcontent.com/pod-product-compliance
Ingram Content Group UK Ltd.
Pitfield, Milton Keynes, MK11 3LW, UK
UKHW022216230426
12048UKWH00016BA/871